AF230707

# Christian Poems, Prayer & Inspirations

## PATRICIA OFFERMAN

Copyright © 2021 by Patricia Offerman

All rights reserved. No part of this publication may be reproduced, distributed, or transmitted in any form or by any means, including photocopying, recording, or other electronic or mechanical methods, without the prior written permission of the publisher, except in the case brief quotations embodied in critical reviews and other noncommercial uses permitted by copyright law.

ISBN:   978-1-63945-023-7 (Paperback)

The views expressed in this book are solely those of the author and do not necessarily reflect the views of the publisher, and the publisher hereby disclaims any responsibility for them.

Writers' Branding
1800-608-6550
www.writersbranding.com
orders@writersbranding.com

# Contents


I've Drawn You to the Father. . . . . . . . . . . . . . . . . . . . . . . .1

Fresh Manna Like the Morning Dew. . . . . . . . . . . . . . . . . . .2

Sufficient Time with Christ . . . . . . . . . . . . . . . . . . . . . . . .3

Adore Me, Don't Ignore Me . . . . . . . . . . . . . . . . . . .4

Purge Our Hearts. . . . . . . . . . . . . . . . . . . . . . . . . .5

Keep Me from Error . . . . . . . . . . . . . . . . . . . . . . . .6

Direct My Steps . . . . . . . . . . . . . . . . . . . . . . . . . .7

God Sent His Only Son. . . . . . . . . . . . . . . . . . . .8

Oh, Treasure of Light and of Love . . . . . . . . . . . . . .9

Lord, Come Quickly . . . . . . . . . . . . . . . . . . . . 10

What a Day of Rejoicing . . . . . . . . . . . . . . . . . . 11

Prayer for Families and Friends. . . . . . . . . . . . . . . 12

Everlasting Father. . . . . . . . . . . . . . . . . . . . . . . 13

Warm the Heart of Others . . . . . . . . . . . . . . . . . 14

He Is Able. . . . . . . . . . . . . . . . . . . . . . . . . . . 15

Walk with Me . . . . . . . . . . . . . . . . . . . . . . . . 16

The Greatest Joys, O Lord . . . . . . . . . . . . . . . . . 17

Refresh Me, Lord . . . . . . . . . . . . . . . . . . . . . . 18

Never Will I Change My Mind . . . . . . . . . . . . . . . 19

Draw upon My Wisdom . . . . . . . . . . . . . . . . . . 20

Sweet Simplicity. . . . . . . . . . . . . . . . . . . . . . . 21

Forgive Our Wasting of Time . . . . . . . . . . . . . . . 22

My Heart Is Your Home . . . . . . . . . . . . . . . . . . 23

Ask Me to Come In. . . . . . . . . . . . . . . . . . . . . 24

He's the Great Promise Keeper. . . . . . . . . . . . . . . 25

Angels of Protection . . . . . . . . . . . . . . . . . . . . 26

Stir Up the Fire . . . . . . . . . . . . . . . . . . . . . . . 27

I Will Walk You Through. . . . . . . . . . . . . . . . . . 28

I Pray for the Multitudes . . . . . . . . . . . . . . . . . . 29

Oh, Worship Him. . . . . . . . . . . . . . . . . . . . . . 30

Always and Forever . . . . . . . . . . . . . . . . . . . . . 31

Let Not Your Heart Be Troubled. . . . . . . . . . . . . . 32

Strong Is Your Bond of Love. . . . . . . . . . . . . . . . 33

Use Your Time Wisely . . . . . . . . . . . . . . . . . . . 34

Come unto Me . . . . . . . . . . . . . . . . . . . . . . . 35

The Straight and Narrow Way . . . . . . . . . . . . . . . 36

Come Fellowship with Jesus . . . . . . . . . . . . . . . . 37

In the Midst of Hardship . . . . . . . . . . . . . . . . . . . . . . . . . . 38
God Always Gives Me His Best . . . . . . . . . . . . . . . . . . . 39
Stand Fast . . . . . . . . . . . . . . . . . . . . . . . . . . . . . . . . . . . . . 40
Lead Me, Oh, Lead Me . . . . . . . . . . . . . . . . . . . . . . . . . . 41
I'll Get You Through . . . . . . . . . . . . . . . . . . . . . . . . . . . 42
An Undivided Heart . . . . . . . . . . . . . . . . . . . . . . . . . . . . 43
Enjoy the Present Moment . . . . . . . . . . . . . . . . . . . . . . 45
The One True Joy . . . . . . . . . . . . . . . . . . . . . . . . . . . . . . 46
Sacred Moments . . . . . . . . . . . . . . . . . . . . . . . . . . . . . . . 47
Ordinary People . . . . . . . . . . . . . . . . . . . . . . . . . . . . . . . 48
It Is Love That Opens Hearts . . . . . . . . . . . . . . . . . . . . 49
Grace Sets One Free . . . . . . . . . . . . . . . . . . . . . . . . . . . . 50
Engaged in Your Own Doings . . . . . . . . . . . . . . . . . . . 51
I Suffered for Your Sorrow . . . . . . . . . . . . . . . . . . . . . . 52
I Shall Never Be Ashamed . . . . . . . . . . . . . . . . . . . . . . 53
Fully Surrendered . . . . . . . . . . . . . . . . . . . . . . . . . . . . . . 54
Do You Know Jesus? . . . . . . . . . . . . . . . . . . . . . . . . . . . 55
Sweet Whispers . . . . . . . . . . . . . . . . . . . . . . . . . . . . . . . . 56
Let Me Be Your Daddy . . . . . . . . . . . . . . . . . . . . . . . . . 57
Tell All the World . . . . . . . . . . . . . . . . . . . . . . . . . . . . . . 59
My Spiritual Bread . . . . . . . . . . . . . . . . . . . . . . . . . . . . . 61
Lasting Peace . . . . . . . . . . . . . . . . . . . . . . . . . . . . . . . . . . 62
I've Never Lived This Moment . . . . . . . . . . . . . . . . . . . 63
As the Time Draws Near to Your Coming . . . . . . . . . . 64
Take My Love, My Worship, Lord . . . . . . . . . . . . . . . . 65
Praises to Your Name . . . . . . . . . . . . . . . . . . . . . . . . . . . 66
My Love for You Will Never End . . . . . . . . . . . . . . . . . 67
Bright as the Sun . . . . . . . . . . . . . . . . . . . . . . . . . . . . . . . 68
Every Moment, Every Minute . . . . . . . . . . . . . . . . . . . . 69
Private Devotions . . . . . . . . . . . . . . . . . . . . . . . . . . . . . . 70
I Grace You with Favor . . . . . . . . . . . . . . . . . . . . . . . . . 71
There's Power in My Name . . . . . . . . . . . . . . . . . . . . . . 72
You're Anxious About Many Things . . . . . . . . . . . . . . . 73
My Worship Never Stops . . . . . . . . . . . . . . . . . . . . . . . . 74
Great Songs of Praise on To You . . . . . . . . . . . . . . . . . 76
Please Stop and Listen . . . . . . . . . . . . . . . . . . . . . . . . . . 77
Take My Love, My Worship, Lord . . . . . . . . . . . . . . . . 78
Walk with Me Each Day . . . . . . . . . . . . . . . . . . . . . . . . . 80
Thoroughly Forgiven . . . . . . . . . . . . . . . . . . . . . . . . . . . 81
I'll Continually Speak of Your Mercy . . . . . . . . . . . . . . 82
I Desire Your Affection . . . . . . . . . . . . . . . . . . . . . . . . . 83

The Stress of Daily Living . . . . . . . . . . . . . . . . . . . . . . . . . . . . . 84
The Mender of Broken Hearts . . . . . . . . . . . . . . . . . . . . . . . . . 85
Jesus, Most Tender Friend . . . . . . . . . . . . . . . . . . . . . . . . . . . . 86
Make Him Your Savior . . . . . . . . . . . . . . . . . . . . . . . . . . . . . . 88
Ask God First . . . . . . . . . . . . . . . . . . . . . . . . . . . . . . . . . . . . . 89
My Hallowed Sanctuary Chair . . . . . . . . . . . . . . . . . . . . . . . . 90
My Desire: Develop You into My Likeness . . . . . . . . . . . . . . . 91
I Cleave to My Jesus . . . . . . . . . . . . . . . . . . . . . . . . . . . . . . . . 92
Be Not Down and Discouraged . . . . . . . . . . . . . . . . . . . . . . . 93
Not My Will but Thine . . . . . . . . . . . . . . . . . . . . . . . . . . . . . . 94
Purify My Soul . . . . . . . . . . . . . . . . . . . . . . . . . . . . . . . . . . . . 95
Take No Fear . . . . . . . . . . . . . . . . . . . . . . . . . . . . . . . . . . . . . 96
Let Him Take Full Possession of Your Life . . . . . . . . . . . . . . . 97
Never Doubt God . . . . . . . . . . . . . . . . . . . . . . . . . . . . . . . . . 98
Birth Pains . . . . . . . . . . . . . . . . . . . . . . . . . . . . . . . . . . . . . . . 99
Balance in Your Life . . . . . . . . . . . . . . . . . . . . . . . . . . . . . . . 100
Wash Me of My Sins . . . . . . . . . . . . . . . . . . . . . . . . . . . . . . 101
Stand Tall in Your Faith . . . . . . . . . . . . . . . . . . . . . . . . . . . . 102
All Three of Us Are as One . . . . . . . . . . . . . . . . . . . . . . . . . . 103
Purify My Motives, Lord . . . . . . . . . . . . . . . . . . . . . . . . . . . 104
Make Yourself Known to Me . . . . . . . . . . . . . . . . . . . . . . . . 105
Why Do You Refuse Me? . . . . . . . . . . . . . . . . . . . . . . . . . . . 106
Lord, Forgive Me, Save Me . . . . . . . . . . . . . . . . . . . . . . . . . 107
Surrender, Trust, and Obey . . . . . . . . . . . . . . . . . . . . . . . . . 108
Cease Thy Mourning . . . . . . . . . . . . . . . . . . . . . . . . . . . . . . 110
I Am a Jealous God . . . . . . . . . . . . . . . . . . . . . . . . . . . . . . . 111
Spirit Within Me . . . . . . . . . . . . . . . . . . . . . . . . . . . . . . . . . 112
I Go to My Quiet Place . . . . . . . . . . . . . . . . . . . . . . . . . . . . 113
You're My Handiwork . . . . . . . . . . . . . . . . . . . . . . . . . . . . . 114
Heal and Make Me Whole . . . . . . . . . . . . . . . . . . . . . . . . . . 115
I'm Not Deaf to Your Cry . . . . . . . . . . . . . . . . . . . . . . . . . . 117
Praise to Your Name . . . . . . . . . . . . . . . . . . . . . . . . . . . . . . 119
Doing Your Work . . . . . . . . . . . . . . . . . . . . . . . . . . . . . . . . 120
Suffering Is Only for a Season . . . . . . . . . . . . . . . . . . . . . . . 122
He Bids You Every Day . . . . . . . . . . . . . . . . . . . . . . . . . . . . 123
Share the Good News with Others . . . . . . . . . . . . . . . . . . . . 124
My Sustaining Grace and Mercy . . . . . . . . . . . . . . . . . . . . . 125
Stay Close to Me, My Child . . . . . . . . . . . . . . . . . . . . . . . . . 126
I'm Learning Every Day . . . . . . . . . . . . . . . . . . . . . . . . . . . . 127
Every Step You Take . . . . . . . . . . . . . . . . . . . . . . . . . . . . . . 128
Hear My Tender Call . . . . . . . . . . . . . . . . . . . . . . . . . . . . . . 130

You Surround Me with Your Love . . . . . . . . . . . . . . . . . . . . . . . 132
The Journey in a Lifetime. . . . . . . . . . . . . . . . . . . . . . . . . . . 134
God's Light Destroys Deception . . . . . . . . . . . . . . . . . . . . . . . 135
May People See and Know . . . . . . . . . . . . . . . . . . . . . . . . . . 136
My Worn, Tattered Bible . . . . . . . . . . . . . . . . . . . . . . . . . . . 137
Feeling Uprooted . . . . . . . . . . . . . . . . . . . . . . . . . . . . . . . 139
Set My Heart Aflame . . . . . . . . . . . . . . . . . . . . . . . . . . . . . 140
Open Wide Your Ears . . . . . . . . . . . . . . . . . . . . . . . . . . . . . 142
A Teachable Heart . . . . . . . . . . . . . . . . . . . . . . . . . . . . . . . 143
I'm in Need of Reconstruction. . . . . . . . . . . . . . . . . . . . . . . . . 144
Every Tender Word You Say . . . . . . . . . . . . . . . . . . . . . . . . . 145
I Will Ever Lead You Back Home . . . . . . . . . . . . . . . . . . . . . . 146
Hold Me Close to Your Heart, Lord . . . . . . . . . . . . . . . . . . . . . 147
Each New Day Is a Blessing . . . . . . . . . . . . . . . . . . . . . . . . . 148
It's Not What's on the Outside . . . . . . . . . . . . . . . . . . . . . . . . 149
When Daily Life Overwhelms Me . . . . . . . . . . . . . . . . . . . . . . 150
With Intercession and Groans . . . . . . . . . . . . . . . . . . . . . . . . 151
Live in the Hope of Tomorrow. . . . . . . . . . . . . . . . . . . . . . . . . 152
Doors of Opportunity . . . . . . . . . . . . . . . . . . . . . . . . . . . . . 153
Recharge My Spiritual Battery . . . . . . . . . . . . . . . . . . . . . . . . 154
Rise Up, Stand Tall, and Don't Give Up . . . . . . . . . . . . . . . . . . 155
Fill Me, O Spirit. . . . . . . . . . . . . . . . . . . . . . . . . . . . . . . . . 156
Though We Stumble . . . . . . . . . . . . . . . . . . . . . . . . . . . . . . 157
Keep Me from the Snares. . . . . . . . . . . . . . . . . . . . . . . . . . . . 158
Drugs Destroy Lives . . . . . . . . . . . . . . . . . . . . . . . . . . . . . . 159
Jesus Is Standing There with You. . . . . . . . . . . . . . . . . . . . . . . 160
I'm Only a Vessel . . . . . . . . . . . . . . . . . . . . . . . . . . . . . . . . 161
When Pain Strikes. . . . . . . . . . . . . . . . . . . . . . . . . . . . . . . . 162
As We Quiet Our Spirits . . . . . . . . . . . . . . . . . . . . . . . . . . . . 163

References for Patricia Offerman Publishing. . . . . . . . . . . . . . . . 165

# I've Drawn You to the Father

I have loved you, oh, my people,
With an everlasting love.
With loving kindness, I've drawn you
To the Father above.

You are priests of the King,
Filled with His wonderful light.
You are acceptable to Him,
Yes, acceptable in His sight.

# Fresh Manna Like the Morning Dew

When you do things in your own strength
You will fail every time
Only in Me
Is where you will find

The provisions you need
Just ask and I will supply
Fresh manna like the morning dew
Eagerly and sufficiently I provide

# Sufficient Time with Christ

Sufficient time with Christ
Is all He asks of us.
Sufficient time with Christ,
Truly is a must.

So take the time with Him,
Know you'll not regret.
Just one hour with God alone
Is time you'll never forget.

# Adore Me, Don't Ignore Me

Child!

I have called thee to adore Me, so "adore," don't "ignore." Pray for the many who have chosen to walk away and ignore My call.

If only they knew what they are missing out on. Too often you lose the urgency of My Son's return. Keep praying! Keep reminding others that Christ will come again! Anyone who has given up or has failed to call on Me shall be left behind! Look to Me always.

Amen.

# Purge Our Hearts

Purge our hearts
With Your fire.
Fill our hearts
With Your desires.
Touch our bodies,
Hearts, and minds.
Help us, Lord,
Be ever kind.
Yes, purge and clean
Our hearts each day
That we may ever
Honor and obey.

# Keep Me from Error

Thank You for Your guidance
In big things and the small
Thank You for taking
Care of it all
You keep me from error
As You lead me home
Your promise to me was
You'd never leave me alone
Oh, thank You for all instructions
For teaching me the way to go
Thank You, Lord, for guiding me
How I love You so!

# Direct My Steps

Holy Spirit,
I ask for divine guidance
And insight… direct my
Steps.
Lead and guide me in all
That I do today.
Help me to be aware
Of the many needs of the
People I encounter.
Give me Your wisdom
For each situation
I face as I minister
To the needs of hurting,
Broken people.

Amen.

# God Sent His Only Son

God sent His only begotten Son
To die upon the Cross.
He paid the price with his blood
To redeem what man had lost.
He paid the price for all sins
To every man on earth,
Bringing man eternal life
Through the second birth.

# Oh, Treasure of Light and of Love

Oh, treasure of light and love
Sweet Jesus from above
Thou art a treasure for sure
Whose love forever endures
As gentle as a sweet dove
Oh, treasure of light and love

# Lord, Come Quickly

As the deer pants for water,
So my heart longs to be
With my Father in heaven.
O Lord, come quickly!
For my homeland is in heaven,
And just beyond the gate
Lies the land of forever...
I can hardly wait!

# What a Day of Rejoicing

What a day of rejoicing
When He comes in the clouds,
His people proclaiming,
In voices so loud,
"This is our God so holy,
The one we've waited for,
He's the one we believe
And will forevermore!"

# Prayer for Families and Friends

Lord,

Thank You for Your blessings and the blessing of Your Son Jesus who came to earth bringing salvation to all mankind, and for the gift of Your unending love toward all that You have made.

Touch the hearts of all men, especially for my family and friends, who do not yet know You… O Lord, grace them that they may come to know You as Savior and Lord of their life, that they may live eternally with You in heaven for all eternity.

Amen.

# Everlasting Father

Everlasting Father
I can run to You anytime
You are ever so gentle
You are ever so kind

Thank You for never changing
For always staying the same
Thank You for Your Son Jesus
Who took my sins, my shame

# Warm the Heart of Others

Warm the life of another
By showing them you care
Warm the heart of another
With an outreach of prayer
Give someone a glimpse of hope
Help brighten up their day
Tell them Jesus loves them
In a special way
Give them a delightful smile
That comes from deep within
Give them love and compassion
That comes from only Him.

# He Is Able

He's able to keep you from falling
Faultless and with great joy
He presents you to the Father
Whether woman, man, girl, or boy!
To the only God, our Savior
His glory and majesty
Through Jesus Christ, our Lord
Who has all power and authority

# Walk with Me

Oh, walk with Me and talk with Me,
This is a daily must—
I've ordered every footstep
All you must do is trust!

# The Greatest Joys, O Lord

Some of the greatest joys, O Lord,
Are the little treasures of life
The charm of all creation You give
That brings my heart delight.

# Refresh Me, Lord

Refresh me, Lord
Gladden my heart
Let it swell with You
For You, O Lord
My God and King
Make each day
Brand new!

# Never Will I Change My Mind

No matter where your path may lead
Remember, I've been there
I've always gone before you
With intercessions and prayers

I am always loving
I am always kind
I love you with all my heart
Never will I change my mind!

# Draw upon My Wisdom

Draw upon My wisdom
Draw upon My peace
Through My Living Word, My Spirit
Your stressful cares will cease
You'll know how to handle
Each crisis that comes your way
With My Holy Spirit's strength
Great peace is yours today

# Sweet Simplicity

With holy reverence
And deep humility,
I come to You, O God
With sweet simplicity
Yielding all that I am
To You, my Lord of all
Submitting unto You, O Lord
The providential call
That You placed upon my life
So long, long ago
That is why I say
I want You to know
That Your unconceivable glory
And all that You are to me
Draws me ever closer
To deeper worship of Thee

# Forgive Our Wasting of Time

Lord, hear our prayer today—
Touch our hearts with Your fire
That Your people, O God, would
burn with Your desire

Forgive our wasting of time
When there's so little time to waste
Help us, Lord, to desire and make up
For our constant worldly haste

# My Heart Is Your Home

My place of safety
Is in You, Lord
Jesus Christ, alone
For You are my Lord,
My sweet Savior
My heart is
forever Your home!

# Ask Me to Come In

Weeping of soul
Does not make you a son
Being good is not enough—
You need to ask Me to come

Come into your heart
As you believe
Confess your sins
That you may fully receive

All that I have for sinners
Who desire to come to Me
I Am He who can wash away
The scales so you can see

# He's the Great Promise Keeper

He's the great promise keeper
Who will never be untrue
Who has never broken a promise
He does what He says He will do
He knows what is best for each of us
No two answers are the same
All we must do is ask Him and
Every promise is ours to claim.

# Angels of Protection

He sends His angels
Wherever you go
There's nothing ahead
He does not know
He's always beside you
Protecting you
From above
With hovering angels
Of His love
At the sound of His
Name
Instantly, He's there
Ever protecting
Ever answering
Your prayers!

# Stir Up the Fire

Surround yourself with people
Throughout your life
 Who can stir up the fire

All those "in Christ."
You know what to do
When the fires going down

Let others challenge you
Don't wear a frown
Don't lose your fire, but

Do what God's called you to do
You need continual sparks
To overcome… it's true!

# I Will Walk You Through

Every fiery circumstance
No matter what it may be
Need not be overwhelming
If you look to Me
You're not alone in your affliction
I'm in the fire with you
You need not be afraid, My child
I will walk you through

# I Pray for the Multitudes

Father God,

I pray for the
  multitudes of people
who know You not.
  Touch their darkened
souls that they may
  truly see You
and Your goodness.
  Grant them Your forgiveness
of sins that they be
  made white as snow.
Give meaning to
  their lives that they
may become aware
  of the true call
upon their lives
  here on earth.

Amen.

# Oh, Worship Him

Oh, worship Him and His greatness
For all He's done for you
Lift your holy hands to Him
For He is ever true

Yes, from the highest mountains
To the beauty of the flowers
All echo His greatness
And His awesome power

# Always and Forever

For always and forever, Lord,

I will praise Your Name

For You are my everlasting Father

Who knows and loves me the same.

There is none like unto You, O Mighty One!

When things start going wrong, I will ever look to You and hide myself in the shadow of Thy wings where I am made safe and sound; where no man can take me, yeah, though He slays me; yet I will praise Him for He fulfills all His gracious promises to me.

# Let Not Your Heart Be Troubled

Let not your heart be troubled
Let not your heart take on fears
Rest only in My love
Daily lend Me your ear

Watch, wait, and resist
The impulse to just run—
Watch, wait, and resist
Trust I Am the Almighty One

# Strong Is Your Bond of Love

Strong is Your bond of love, Lord,
In which my hope stands firm
Help me to never forget and
A heart that ever wants to learn

To remain sinless in Your sight
No matter what age I am at
That Your great fidelity is firm
Throughout my entire past

It is my desire, Lord,
To remain sinless before You
Obeying Your Word
For Your Word is ever true

# Use Your Time Wisely

Each one of us, God has given
A twenty-four-hour day
Do you use it wisely,
Or squander it away?

Don't let the days fly past you
And never hesitate
For we live a life of uncertainty
Tomorrow may come too late

Use the day and make it count
Enjoy every moment you have
Do something special for someone
Smile and say a prayer for one who is sad

# Come unto Me

Sacred moments
Sacred times
In My
Holy place—
How I treasure
Our sacred times
As I seek you
Face to face!
Come, My child
Come unto Me
Come daily, My child
Come and see—
First in your life
Is where I should be

# The Straight and Narrow Way

How can we still have joy
When problems haven't changed?
It's by knowing who God is
That our lives are rearranged.

It was He who turns our darkness
Into a brilliant light
Who taught us to trust
In Him
He is our hearts' delight.

Yes, joy, unspeakable joy
Is what we can have each day,
If we've chosen to live our lives
The straight and narrow way.

# Come Fellowship with Jesus

Come fellowship with Jesus
Every day for just an hour,
And soon you'll experience
His glorious awesome power.

Jesus said, "Deny the flesh
Bare your cross come follow me,
I'm the Living God
Who created thee."

"So deny the flesh
Let go of all and let me,
Be your Living God
Who died to set you free."

# In the Midst of Hardship

In the midst of hardship
And great pain
Rise above, my child
And much will be gained

An abundance of a joyous heart
Throughout your day
Untold blessings
Will come your way

So rise above, O child of mine
Let go of every care
My faithfulness and love for you
Will always be there

# God Always Gives Me His Best

God will always lead us
He's always on our side
Working for our good
With His arms opened wide

In good times and bad times
Through times of great distress
We need not worry what to do
For God always gives us His best

# Stand Fast

Stand fast and full of courage, my child
Wherever you choose to go
Allow me to show you new ways
In which your spirit may grow
Allow me the time to lovingly give you
A new word or hope for the day
Stand fast in My love
And in all of My ways

# Lead Me, Oh, Lead Me

Lead me, oh, lead me
By the moment each day
That I may ever
Know Thy will and way
Though trials will come
I depend only on You
For Your Word promises
You shall walk me through

# I'll Get You Through

To bring forth growth
Changes are things you must face
Changes are never easy, you see
Tis hard, but, child, with My grace
You can overcome anything
That you put your mind to
Step back, take My hand,
For have I not promised I'd get you through?

# An Undivided Heart

Thank you, Lord, that
You abound in love
To all who
Call upon You.
Today, dear Lord,
Give me an
Undivided heart
That I may love You
And serve You to
The best of my ability.
Grant me Your strength
And Your grace
As I go about my day.
Give me a sign
Of Your great goodness
In all that I do, as I
Follow Your leading
 And plan for my path.
May I magnify and
Glorify Your Son Jesus
In all I do and say.

May the light of
Your goodness reach out
To those You put
Into my path
May Your light and image
Draw them through
This vessel of Your love,
As Your Spirit leads
And guides my steps,
For I am Your vessel—
Do as You please with me.
Use me as Your
Voice, hands, and feet
Bringing glory to Your
Holy Name

# Enjoy the Present Moment

Look to the future
 Look to the future—
Is what the world
 would say,
But if your focus is
 Always the future,
You'll miss the glory
 Of today!
A constant futuristic attitude
 Brings your soul anxiety,
Which brings you down the path
 Of frailty!
Now man can plan ahead
 His whole entire life,
And end up with nothing
 But heartache and strife.
So I exhort you strongly,
 Live one day at a time,
Enjoy the present moment
 Or you'll miss the divine!

# The One True Joy

He who brings
      Great joy to our hearts
Is the one true joy
      Only He can impart
For no other joy
In all the earth
      Can give great joy
Through the gift of His birth
      For He lavished His love
Upon us that day
      Bringing salvation
      In a miraculous way

# Sacred Moments

Sacred moments in the quiet place
      Is where I'd like you to be
For I treasure our time together
      Oh, how it delights Me.
I desire all of you, my child
      As your Father, I deserve the best
Come… body, mind, and spirit
      In My chamber, you'll find sweet rest.
So take some time each morning
      In the beginning of your day
To hear your Father's voice
      As I lead the path of your way.

# Ordinary People

Ordinary people,
  Ordinary people
    My people of the past,
     My people of today
All were and are
  Ordinary people
   I use
   In extraordinary ways
It's ordinary people
  Like you, My child
    That I choose
     All the time
The broken earthen vessels
  Are chosen because
    In them, My
     Light can shine.
Yes, broken vessels
  Of My choosing
    Vessels that are
     Put to the test
Through fires, trials,
  Tribulations
    Are the ones who
  Work out best.

# It Is Love That Opens Hearts

It is love that opens hearts
And as an ambassador of Mine
I ask that your heart be open
That I may use you in My time
To bring others to Me
Through your compassion, your love
That others may come
Knowing My love from above
That freely flows from your living heart
That I've freely given to you
So you may love and show them
As My Spirit walks them through
Every trial or oppression
Every sin, every strife
Lead them and tell them
How to have true life
There is no fear in love
Perfect love casts out all fear
Fear involves torment
I am made perfect in love when God is near
Openly and completely Lord
Come, take My life, I give it to you
Take Me and use Me
In all you ask Me to do

# Grace Sets One Free

Are yesterday's mistakes
Holding you down?
Don't get discouraged
Don't wear a frown

For God's grace is yours
And grace is free
He'll bestow upon you
What He's bestowed upon me

His grace, oh, wonderful grace
Was not in vain, you know
God's wonderful grace
Will help you to grow

And so become
All you can be
The grace of God
Sets one free

# Engaged in Your Own Doings

How it grieves My Spirit when
you withdraw from Me
And my call
So often you seem so
engaged in your own
doings and have an attitude
of "I'm too busy,
So don't bother me, God,
as my schedule is
very busy today."
My child, your schedule
is busy every day and
Worsens as the weeks go by.
When will you learn, my
Little one, that it will only
Worsen if you continue to put
Everything before Me?
Come, my child, put Me first by
drawing near Me daily
I have a "reserved" sign at your spot!
You're welcome anytime

# I Suffered for Your Sorrow

If hearts were never broken
How could I ever mend
All the shattered hearts and minds
Of My servants and My friends?

I am the man of sorrows
Who heals those in despair,
but how can I heal anyone
Or work and repair?

If you never run into My arms
To take away all fears,
Child, do you not know
I've counted every tear?

I suffered for your sorrows
And became a victim soul
All because I love you
And want to see you whole

# I Shall Never Be Ashamed

I shall never
Be ashamed nor
Stop praising and shouting
Out Your glorious Name!
How I love You, my Lord
My God and Savior
Of my soul
I will shout it to
the sky and earth
Because no one else
Seems to want to hear!
How sad to know
That people are so
Reserved, restrained, and
Inhibited
And even ashamed
To fully praise You
As You truly deserve.
Lord, how I await
The freedom of
Heaven on earth
To be able to greet
And shout great glories
Out to You spontaneously
Glorifying You throughout my days! Halleluiah

# Fully Surrendered

The Lamb reigns amid the praises
of His ransomed ones
He alone is holy
God's one and only Son
Ever enthroned in glory
His love so sweet, so tender,
Comes to those who have
Fully surrendered
S-urrender to the
U-tmost High God, the one who was
R-esurrected and fully
R-aised from the dead, who
E-nlivens every soul,
N-o matter the color of their skin—He
D-ied for one and all
E-ntering into heaven on the third day.
R-emember, He is the author of
E-ternal life
D-on't waste time, surrender today!

# Do You Know Jesus?

Though you go
       To church
One day of
       the week
You give God
       your tithes
To neighbors
You speak
You help when
You're needed
You sing in
       A choir
You're gentle
       and kind . . .
But do you
       Know Jesus?
Has your life
       Been restored—
By inviting Him in
       As your Savior
          And Lord?

# Sweet Whispers

Oh, how my spirit
    Leaps and prances
With great exultation—
    My spirit dances
When You whisper and assure me
    Of Your great love
From Your golden gilded throne
    High above
Oh, how I worship You
    My Lord and my King
Oh, how my heart
    So jubilantly sings
As Your sweet whispers
    Breathe into my ear:
"My precious child,
    I am ever near."

# Let Me Be Your Daddy

Let Me hold
Your hand, son
I'll keep you
From your sins
Please don't
Walk away, son
Just ask Me
To come in.
I promise you
My loving comfort
I'll be your
Very best friend
Allow me to
Walk you through
For this is
Not the end
I knew you
I formed you
Before the
Beginning of time
I called you

Long ago
So you could
Be all Mine
So let Me be
Your Daddy, and
The path
I chose for you
You need not
ever worry, son
My love is
Ever true

# Tell All the World

Go out and tell the world
Go out share the gift of My Son.
Go out to share the gospel
Of the great and Mighty One

Share with them the gift
The greatest gift you can give
Share the gift of My Son
That they may eternally live

Never stop telling them of Me
Never let a day go by
Never waste a fleeting moment
For tomorrow that person could die

Yes, tell them I Am waiting
Tell them I Am at the door
How I desire them to call on Me
To live with Me forevermore

How many hearts can you enlighten?
How many hearts can you cheer?
How many souls can you help,
Just in one short year?

So go out and tell all the world
Go tell them of My Son
Sharing the truth of My gospel
Sharing how Christ shall come

# My Spiritual Bread

When the load is far too heavy to bear
God lifts my load and carries me there
He strengthens my faith
As I call on Him in prayer
My God is the answer
What's best for me He knows
No matter what He asks of me
Or where He leads me to go
For He is ever faithful
He is ever so true
In the hour of my trials
He strengthens and enables me to do
All that needs to get done
In the days ahead
He gives me His strength
And my spiritual daily bread.

# Lasting Peace

Thank you, Lord, for the peace in my heart
That I can have every day
The kind of peace that is lasting
A peace that no one can take away.
Though I have many trials and testings
And at times I'd like to shout,
Yet I know, my sweet Jesus
This I know without doubt:
That as I abide in my Jesus
So tenderly loving and kind,
My troubles seem to fall away
Because of Jesus, so sweet, so divine.
Thou art wonderful and glorious
My sweet Savior and my King
Thou art the only one
Who makes my heart sing.

# I've Never Lived This Moment

I've never lived
    this moment before,
And I'll never
    live it again,
So I ask, Dear Lord,
    that I live it well,
That You lead my day
    from beginning to end.

Heavenly Father,

Thank You for these moments with You as I start my day.

# As the Time Draws Near to Your Coming

As the time draws near to Your coming
The trials become greater each day
Yet I know if my focus is You, Lord
If I trust in what You say
I know that I will make it through
The trials, the tribulations
If I look not to the right nor the left
But look straight unto You, my salvation
For You are the author and the finisher of my faith
To whom I've loved and given my heart
I will not fail nor succumb to the terror
For You alone are my rampart
Yes, I will put all my trust in You
Though the mountains be cast in the sea
My hope is in You, Lord, always
Thus, I will know You take care of me
I'll not worry nor take on fears
But will go about my way
Waiting for the trumpets call
For that glorious resounding day.

# Take My Love, My Worship, Lord

Take my life, my praises
Take my worship and movements unto You
Take all of me, Sweet Jesus, my Lord
From Your child's heart, ever so true
Who loves You more than I can express
Oh, words can no longer explain
The great fire, the desire, the pleasure I get
You are my life, my eternal flame!

Yes, there is none like You
None, none like You, the Christ
You are my very essence—
That gave my darkened heart great light
O God, how I adore You
Into Your gates, I'll ever bring
All that I am, all that I can be
Yes, I bow down and sing

# Praises to Your Name

Your Name is above all names,
>You're the way, the truth, and the light
You're the resurrection—
>Who wears a robe of white

You are Shekhinah Glory—
>You're more brilliant than the sun
You are the son of David—
>God's only begotten one

You're the Horn of Salvation
>A banner lifted high
Rivers of Living Water—
>Master and Rabbi

Lord, You're the quickening spirit
>To the lost and lonely heart
You're the great physician
>And healing is Your art

You're the mighty warrior
>The Glory of Israel
The everlasting Father
>The Maker of heaven and hell.

# My Love for You Will Never End

Let My new song arise in you
In your broken wounded heart
Listen to My soft still voice
As I give you a new start

I Am your strength and salvation
I Am your music, your song
Look unto Me, your salvation
Rejoice and sing all day long

My music is ever playing
So sing praises again and again
Let it calm your spirit, oh, child
My love for you shall never end

# Bright as the Sun

Bright as the sun is His face
Blazing are His eyes of fire
The light of His face shines brightly
Drawing people to hunger and desire

Asking Him into their heart
Making Him their Savior and King
Repenting of all their sins
Falling down before Him to sing

Glory, halleluiah
Glory to Jesus, our King
Glory, halleluiah
We bow before You and sing

# Every Moment, Every Minute

Every moment, every minute
History's changing fast
Times have changed
The good times won't last

So what are you waiting for?
The times are very clear
That the day of Christ
Is ever so near

Don't wait for tomorrow
For tomorrow may never come
Don't miss out on God's
Glorious Savior and Son.

# Private Devotions

You must have a listening attitude
And the right frame of mind
Not being in a rush or hurry
But taking and giving Me time
As you have private devotions
Taking daily time for prayer
By interceding for others
Showing how much you care
It takes a prayerful quiet spirit
And a desire to be taught
Ever seeing the heart of God
Seeking Him in your thoughts

# I Grace You with Favor

I grace you with favor, child
In everything I bring your way
Receive and accept it, My child
My graces are new each day

I'll fulfill all My promises
If you'll only believe,
Never allowing the enemy
To come to deceive.

Be encouraged and know I love you
My promises I will fulfill
Just trust, obey me, My child
Hush now… be still!

# There's Power in My Name

There is power in My Name
So speak My Name
Speak My Name
There's power in My Name
Speak My Name
Demons will scatter
Thunder will clatter
So speak the power of My Name
Speak My Name with gratitude
It will change your attitude
Just by speaking My Name

# You're Anxious About Many Things

You're anxious
   about many things
Forget all of that—
   just praise Me and sing.
Pour out your heart.
   let go of all pride
Humble yourself
   put everything aside
Look unto Me,
   be not afraid
For I'll fulfill
   the promises I made.

# My Worship Never Stops

My worship never stops with you, Lord,
It goes on and on each day;
Never ever stopping, Lord,
As I worship You night and day.

My heart never stops singing and crying,
Great praises that come from deep within;
Glorifying and worshipping at all times,
Because in You, I am sure and without sin.

Not a day or a moment goes by—
When I'm not thinking about You,
O Lord God, Almighty One—
How do people ever live without You?

I love You, I love You, I love You!
You are everything to me.
In and throughout my whole day,
You're all I think on and see!

If this is what its like here on earth,
My, what shall heaven be like?
Oh, what wonderful days we will have
Praising, dancing in Your glorious light!

O Lord, it's so hard to wait—
When all that I think and I do
Is wallow and dance in great delight
Just praising and worshipping You!

# Great Songs of Praise on To You

Great songs of praises on to You!
All of my days and my nights;
I believe that's why You made me
So I'll just continue to fully delight—
In You, my Lord, my Maker,
Who desires me to fully hide
Under the wings of Your covering, Lord
I will ever praise and abide
Just like the angels in heaven
Who praise and worship You all day
I know this is how you made me, dear Lord
Happy and delighted in all of Your ways.

# Please Stop and Listen

There's an important message
I don't want you to miss
And I know there are some
Who don't want to hear this
But I must speak
And I must obey
So please stop and listen
What I have to say
That Jesus, yes, He's coming
His great coming is very near
In this message of love from Him,
Jesus tells us not to fear—
Now if you don't know Jesus,
You've not asked Him into your heart,
Call upon His Name and believe
From evil men, He'll set you apart
He's called on you so often
Yet so often you chose not to hear
But I, as an apostle, cry to you
Jesus is very, very near!
It takes but a moment.
To confess all your sins
Call on Jesus Christ
Ask Him to come in.

# Take My Love, My Worship, Lord

I love You, O Lord,
My Savior, my King;
I worship You, Lord,
Above everything.
For you are the Lord
Who formed all earth;
 You are the one
Who gave me new birth.
What more can I ask?
What more can I say?
Except worship, praise You
Exalt You all day.

Oh, you are "King of my heart,"
Yes, Lord, only You—
You are my whole life,
There is nothing and no one like You!
You are everything—everything
Everything to me
When I look into Your face
There is nothing and no one other than Thee
O Lord, how this child loves You,
Without You, life would not be;
I come, I bow, I worship, I sing,
"Thou art all to me!"

You're the first thing I turn to
Each morning of my day;
Giving You great honor
Seeking Your will and
All of Your ways
Standing in Your presence
O Lord, my servant, my King
What more can I say, Lord?
You're my all, my everything

# Walk with Me Each Day

You'll learn to walk victoriously
As you walk with Me each day
Hear My voice listen carefully
To what I teach and say

For I speak to each of my children
Yet so many do not hear
Will you be one who listens
And holds My Words dear?

I have a call upon your life
Trust My ways instead
Follow Me, My precious child
I'm always one step ahead

Leading you and guiding you
I'll go to any length—
All you must do, My child,
Is trust in Me and My strength

Yes, the call I have for you
Will take a bit of time,
But if you trust and obey—
I promise, you'll be fine

# Thoroughly Forgiven

Let go of all the stories
That happened way back when
I do not give you permission,
To view them once again!

All things from your past
I said would be made new,
You need not go back there, child,
For I am healing you!

Have forgiveness in your heart
For those who did you wrong.
When you thoroughly forgive, my child,
You shall have a new song!

You're on a healing journey
As I make You whole
Allow Me, your Jesus, to cleanse
Your being, mind, and soul.

I will be the one who decides
When I desire to reveal
Things that happened long ago
Through My Word that heals!

# I'll Continually Speak of Your Mercy

I will praise the Lord
no matter what happens to me,
I'll continually speak of Your mercy
And Your grace that sets me free

Yes… continually, I will offer
A sacrifice of praise
For taking all my scarlet sins
And washing them away

Though my heart was dark
Now it's full of light
Because of Your great favor
My heart is ever bright

# I Desire Your Affection

Oh, My children,
My little children,
Do you not know
How much
I love you?
How I would enjoy
Intimate conversations
With you or just
To have you quiet
Before Me at my throne?
I created you for
Myself… how I
Desire… how I
Desire your love,
Affection, and obedience
Put all else aside
Come be with Me daily

# The Stress of Daily Living

Are you disappointed?
  Has sickness hit you today?
Are finances stretched to the max?
  Have your kids gone astray?

Problems with cars and appliances,
  Troubles with the neighbor's boy—
Is the stress of daily living
  Robbing you of joy?

Then… Call upon the Lord
  He's someone you can trust
Roll your cares on Him—
  This is a must
Commit your way to the Lord
  Trust also in Him,
And He shall bring it to pass—
  His victory you'll win
Don't look at your problems,
  Look straight into His face—
He will help to strengthen you
  Giving you His grace

# The Mender of Broken Hearts

He's the mender of broken hearts
Of simple men and kings
He hears the deepest cries
Of worship as we sing

He knows and feels your pain
He hears your cry of despair
Try to remember He will never
Give us more than we can bear

He's attuned to every need we have
With compassionate sensitivity
Because of the loving Father
Who is kind and always will be

# Jesus, Most Tender Friend

O Jesus, most tender friend
Breathe upon this child
As I awaken
To a new day to love,
Honor, and worship You
In all I think, do, or say.
Your sweet whisperings
Of love and grace
Awaken an even deeper desire
To please You;
My sweet Master and my King;
Your presence within me
Enlivens and enriches
My soul as You and
Your light,
Love and blessings,
And Your Word imbues
My spirit,
For I am Your child,
Your lamb,
Your little one
Who humbly desires

To please You in
Every way
Take this day
And all that is unfolded
In this moment of time
For it is Your day
Do with me as You please

Amen.

# Make Him Your Savior

The God that saved
        the upright in heart—
Can save your soul
        and set you apart…
Apart from the world
        and all that's within—
Make Jesus your Savior
        By asking Him in!
The task is so simple…
        and all you must do—
Is confess with your mouth
        that He died just for you
Then believe in your heart
        that from death, He was raised…
Repent of your sins,
        and then you'll be saved!

# Ask God First

Sometimes I am preoccupied
And my thoughts just tune You out
Sometimes I'm in a whirlwind
Sometimes I even shout
I sometimes am stiff-necked
Sensing a hardened heart
At times I am prideful
Thinking I'm so smart!
Assuming You are with me
Yet I never asked You to
Then I wonder why
I'm so down, so blue!
Then I go right on serving
Before I've even prayed
Never really asking, confiding,
Nor listening to You, I'm afraid!
So, Lord, I'm sorry, help me
To communicate first with You
That I may do only those things
Only what You, Lord, called me to do!

# My Hallowed Sanctuary Chair

My hallowed sanctuary chair
Is where I like to be
My chair reserved for praying
Humbling myself unto Thee
There You give me such
Rest and peace
When I give all things to You
And fully release
Everything about my love for You
Then Your Words Your light appears
And I hear Your sweet whisper
"I love you, my dear"
I spend hours before You
Daily in Your presence I come
Where I am fed Your Word
And blessed by both Father and Son
As You speak so tenderly
Into my ear right there
Speaking of Your love, Your light
As I'm waiting in my sanctuary chair
O Lord God—not one
Single day can I go or be away
For when I don't have time with You
Nothing goes well that day!

# My Desire: Develop You into My Likeness

My child—
My desire is to fully and
Completely develop you
Into my likeness
So that in this
Life, you will
Lack nothing
I am firm in my love and in
Teaching and training you
As one of my soldiers
So rise up to the call
I want you to be
Steadfast,
Confident,
Firm in my all,
Encompassing love,
Able and ready
To walk uprightly
Through all situations,
So you, in turn, may
Give the same sympathy,
Love, and compassion
To others in the same
Way I have given
Unto you.

# I Cleave to My Jesus

I cleave to my Jesus
I have faith and great trust
He gives me great hope
For hope is a must

He is always looking after me
Day after day
He's my strong tower
What more can I say?

My heart, my soul
Shall never frown
With my faith in Him
I shall not get down

For He supplies me
With His great strength
He gives me the ability
To go to great lengths

In the race,
I'm in it to win
Because of my Jesus
Who lives within.

# Be Not Down and Discouraged

Do not be down
And discouraged, my soul
My hope is in God
Soon I shall be whole

Though all my life,
Sickness has been my cross
This too is my gain
And not for loss

For I know all things
Go through His hand
It is not to harm me
But it is in His plans

For what the devil meant for bad
God turns it for good
Yeah, I will still praise Him
Just as I should

For nothing shall stop me
From ever praising Him
For I know in the end
He says I win!

# Not My Will but Thine

Not my will but Thine, Lord
Thy will shall be done
Strengthen me by Your Spirit
And Your Mighty Son

Lord, I'll serve with all my heart
I'll go to any length
Please give me Your comforting love
And Your Spirit's strength

That I may fully do Your will
I will obey
Strengthen me daily, Lord
This I ask and pray

# Purify My Soul

Strengthen my faith, make me whole
Purify my entire soul
Deep within my spirit, I pray
Strengthen me, Lord, more each day

When I start to waiver
Touch me with Your favor
Open my eyes that I may see
Touch my heart, set me free

# Take No Fear

Don't be afraid of the dark,
Nor fear the dangers of the day
Nor dread the plagues of darkness,
Nor disaster that comes your way.

For the Lord will keep you safe,
You can lie down and sleep in peace
He surely will shelter you
Let all fear of danger cease.

All His faithful promises are true,
He'll never let you stumble or fall
He ever watches over you,
If on Him you will call.

Yes… Jehovah Himself is caring for you,
He wants you to know
He keeps his eye upon you,
As you come and go!

# Let Him Take Full Possession of Your Life

When we fully yield to the Lord
Knowing Him intimately
Allowing Him full possession
He moves us by His Spirit, giving opportunities
To be a true witness for Him
Saying "yes" to the call
You need His powerful Spirit
As you testify to all;
He leads and fully does the work
Through His servants' hands
As we are led fully by Him
For the divine purpose of His plans.

# Never Doubt God

I never doubt God
He is always there
He'll meet your every need
If you call on Him in prayer
He's there waiting
Waiting just for you
So ask and believe
That He can do—
Whatever it takes—
I tell you, my friend
God answers prayers
His mercy never ends
So call on Him today
He's just waiting for you
To ask Him in prayer
With a heart that's true
Don't be afraid
He calls us friends
Just ask in faith
And an answer He will send

# Birth Pains

O Lord,
I sense in my spirit
More and more each day
We are at the beginning of birth pains
Before Christ comes to take us away.

In my spirit, do I

travail and groan

Longing for You, my Lord

To come take us home

# Balance in Your Life

My child, you need to learn
To have balance in your life
Balance in every area
Will keep you out of strife
Then My peace shall rest on you
Not just by chance—
My peace shall be yours, my child
In every circumstance
So keep all things in balance
Then this you can be sure
That you, my child, shall be kept
Ever safe, ever secure
Under the covering of My shadow—
The shadow of My wings—
Allowing perfect balance to become
Part of your life in everything!

# Wash Me of My Sins

Wash me of my sins, O Lord
Oh, wash me once again.
Renew my wayward spirit,
With Your presence once again
Yes, wash me, cleanse me, Lord
I want to make amends
Revive me with sweet joy
Again and again and again!

# Stand Tall in Your Faith

My child, stand tall in your faith, steadfast and sure, never doubting My Word and what I'm asking of you, my child.

Grow not impatient but adamant in obedience, as I teach you how to be consistent and firm, standing in the areas I show you.

I'll teach you how to press in and press on to the goal I have set for you. It takes a willingness of heart and spirit, one that will not give in to the whims of the evil one.

Amen.

# All Three of Us Are as One

Look up, look up…
Do not fear
My grace is sufficient
I Am ever here

Look to My Father
Look unto the Son
Call upon My Spirit
All three of Us are as one

# Purify My Motives, Lord

Purify my motives, Lord
Burn away useless thoughts You see
You are my consuming fire
Rid me of useless deeds.

Purify, consume me, Lord
Redeem my rebellion and tears
Thank You, Lord, for redeeming
All of my wasted years.

# Make Yourself Known to Me

O Lord, make Yourself known to me in an even greater way. How I love to bring honor to Your Name as You bring the people You desire me to speak to, into my path, that need the light of Your truth, encouragement, and great hope. Oh, that they would know and recognize the wonderful truth of You!

Yes, I love You, thank You for choosing me as Your vessel. I am honored to be Yours and used as You please with no limitations!

I love You, Abba!

Love, Your little one

# Why Do You Refuse Me?

Oh, precious child
Who chooses to stand alone
My arms are opened wide
So heaven can be your home
Why do you pull back?
Why do you live in sorrow?
Why do you always
Think and say tomorrow?
Do you not realize
That I Am all you need?
I Am He who supplies
Oh, come, my child, I plead
Daily you must come
To fully hear My cries
When I took upon every sin
The day I died
So you could have eternal life
So you could be My son
Why is it that you daily refuse
The Savior, the Mighty One?
If you only knew
The love I have for you
My powerful love
That can touch and fully renew
Come, come, my son—
Let Me save thee
From thyself and others
Please come, I'll set you free.

# Lord, Forgive Me, Save Me

I have been
Living in horrible sin
O Lord, forgive me
Please take me in.
I know I've ignored You
Most all of my life
I see my way of living
Just causes me strife
Forgive me for putting You
Off every day—
Today I see the light
I want it Your way
Please forgive me
Of all that I've done
I ask of You, Lord,
To give me Your Son
Pour out Your mercy
Upon this soul
Touch, heal, restore
Make me whole.

# Surrender, Trust, and Obey

Has the joy of your "first love" departed?
Is peace and rest far from you?
Are you feeling parched like a desert
In everything you do?

Have you forgotten "my yoke is easy"?
That your soul must yield to obey
Remember, I, the Lord, give you the strength
You need for each day.

To abide in Me, you need to surrender
To surrender all is to obey and trust
To lean wholly upon Me and yield
To be still and rest is a must!

Come… there is a place of safety
Where peace and rest are sure;
A place of sure victory,
A place where you're secure

That place is a haven, the heart of My Son
Is ever open to thee
That's where you'll find your true rest
Where you learn to abide in Me.

Abiding is the work of My Spirit
It's not something that you do
So… surrender, trust, and obey
Let My Spirit do its work in you!

# Cease Thy Mourning

Cease thy mourning,
Oh, man of sin,
Christ made a way
For you to win.
All you must do
Is call on His Name.
He is ever near,
So proclaim,
"I need You, Jesus,
To come into my heart.
I've sinned against You,
And I need a new start.
I've gone down the wrong road,
Please come in,
Into my heart, as
I confess all my sins.
I'm so sorry, Lord,
I've gone my own way.
Will You forgive me
And save me today?"

# I Am a Jealous God

I am a jealous God.
I desire you all to Myself.
Child, please come to Me.
Don't put Me in a dark corner shelf.

Empty yourself of the worldly,
Come unto Me each day,
Close the door behind you,
Come listen to what I say.

I've so much to teach you;
In the days ahead,
Trust and believe in Me
And in all that I've said.

Allowing Me daily time with you,
Know your prayers avail;
By putting Me first,
Your prayers will never fail.

# Spirit Within Me

Spirit of God within me…
Make me patient and kind,
Help me to do Your will,
And give me peace of mind.

Help me to always be humble
In all the things I do…
Help me to love You completely,
Surrendering my life to You!

Let my heart keep yearning…
For more and more of You.
Make me to be obedient
And ever so true.

Never let me wander
From Your everlasting arms…
Keep me from the "worldly"
And all that does me harm!

Give me compassion and mercy…
For those who do me wrong…
Give me a brand new life
And my heart a whole new song!

# I Go to My Quiet Place

I go to my quiet place
Where all is calm and still
With great joy, gladness—
Where I seek Thy perfect will
Yes, my hallowed place
There in my favorite chair
Where daily I come to bow
With all my tools, I gather there—
My Bible, my books—
My paper and pens
Waiting for Your Word
Your whispers—when
You gently speak
And tell me to begin
To intercede to write a poem
Or perhaps to confess my sins
To pray for other people
And the world's news of the day
Yes, daily I come, Lord,
To lift You up and to praise

# You're My Handiwork

You're my handiwork, my treasure,
Fashioned by my hand in every way.
I'm changing you into My image
Day by day by day.

Do not be discouraged, my child.
It takes a great deal of time
To fashion and reshape you
Into an image like Mine.

I'll allow you to go through experiences
And trials galore,
But you'll come out shining
And loving Me even more.

If you'll have faith and trust Me
As I challenge you to…
Stand upon and test My Word,
Proving it to be true.

Yes, you've been preordained
To bring glory to My Name,
Drawing others to Me
Through My Holy Spirit's flame.

# Heal and Make Me Whole

Underneath my sins, O God,
Lies great hardness of heart.
Give me the grace
To see the truth,
Give a brand new start.

Forgive my wandering,
My running
In the opposite way,
The awful things
I've done, Lord,
And things I still say.

Dig deeper into my heart, Lord,
Dig deeper into my soul.
Bring renewal of heart,
Heal and make
Me whole.

I realize now my
Worldly ways
Kept me far from
Your will.
I repent and desire
If You'll have me still—

Forgive me for denying You
And Your loving Son.
Help me, Lord,
Forgive me
Lead me to
Your Holy One
Amen.

# I'm Not Deaf to Your Cry

I'm not deaf to your cry.
My compassion never ends.
Call upon Me.
I'll be your friend.
So call upon Me
And My precious Name.
Release all your cares.
Take on no shame.
For I love you, my child.
Please invite Me into your heart.
Let go of the struggles.
All fears will depart.
My arms are outstretched,
Fully opened wide,
Just waiting for you
To ask Me inside.
Allow Me to come in,
Drawing closer to you,
 That I may restore
And make you like new.
My faithfulness is great,
My mercy new every morn.

Just ask and believe
And become reborn.
Real life begins
And ends with Me.
I'm the beginning.
I am the end.
Oh, don't you see?

# Praise to Your Name

Sing to the Lord each morning.
Give praise to His Mighty Name.
Adoration, praise, and glory,
His blessings proclaim.

For He is the Lord Almighty,
The magnificent Holy One,
Who was and is and always will be,
Whose victory has come.

To break the bondage
Of sin in the earth,
To break down the wall
That were there at our birth.

Oh, He is the victor,
The battle His alone…
He is the only man
Whose blood can atone.
Oh, ascribe to the Lord.
Be glad and rejoice.
Lift up your hands
And sing with your voice.

Hosanna, Hosanna, Hosanna,
I give praise to Your Mighty Name.
Praise, honor, and glory,
Your Word, I proclaim.

# Doing Your Work

Diligently, faithfully, obediently, Lord,
I give my life to You.
Help me stay faithful to my call
And what You've called me to do.

May I always treasure the moment
And the opportunities You give
That I may ever serve You
Each day that I live.

As I depend upon
Your great strength, Your grace,
And Your Holy Spirit power
For all that I must face.

Those I minister and love on,
All those You send my way,
As I lay my hands on each one,
Bowing my head to pray.

For guidance of Your Spirit,
Your great wisdom from the start;
Ministering to those You bring
By sharing and doing my part.

Sharing the "good news" of salvation
And Your wonderful plans
That You, O Lord, so freely give
To each and every man.

# Suffering Is Only for a Season

Be conscious of My love
In the midst of suffering.
My grace is sufficient
And takes away the sting.

The things you're enduring now
At the moment are hard to bear,
But it's only for a season,
So do not despair.

For the very thing you're going through,
Someday I'll use for My glory;
You'll be helping others
By your testimony and story.

So look to Me, My child,
Be conscious of My love,
Lift your hands and spirit
To your Father high above.

# He Bids You Every Day

Jesus Christ, the
Father's only Son,
Bids you every day
To call… When He says, Come,
Be not a stranger,
Just open up the door,
And you shall have
Life forevermore!
Call upon His Name,
For great joy shall be yours.
He is the one who
Revives and fully He restores!

# Share the Good News with Others

Share the good news with others
Share it beyond all measure
For My good news you share
Is like a newfound treasure

Do not hoard it for yourself
But share your great wealth with them
It is My true love you give away
So do it over and over again

Use every opportunity
To tell of My greatness, My power
Waste not one moment
Do not waste an hour

Tell them how much I love them
And how deeply I care
Please pray for the entire world
In your everyday prayers

# My Sustaining Grace and Mercy

It is by My sustaining grace and mercy that you exist, My child. My grace and My mercy uphold you through the hard and rocky places. Do not give up, and do not give in, but stay strong. Trust Me and know that My sustaining grace is yours. Never doubt that, for I sustain all who have made Me their Savior and Lord. All things, no matter how bad they look, are under My control. Do not lose hope, but trust in Me, knowing that it shall be well with your soul. Victory shall be yours if you do not give in to the devil's lies and defeat. Put him in his place and continue to trust fully in Me, oh, precious one. I am with you always.

Your Loving Father

# Stay Close to Me, My Child

Stay close to me, my child
Let the light of your heart shine bright
 I will soon return for My church
But not 'til the time is just right

Keep on doing what you're doing
Watch with anticipation for the groom
Watch over your heart, stay far from sin
And you'll not be sons of doom

For I have prepared a place for you
A mansion will soon be your home
You shall live an eternity of joy
You will never ever walk alone

So be prepared, be ready
Obedient, pure, and kind
Only the bridegroom of your heart
Knows the exact moment of time

You must always be ready
With your heart always right
Looking to the eastern sky
In the clouds and rays of light

# I'm Learning Every Day

He's making me righteous in His sight
Teaching me how to live in the light
No more darkness… no more sin—
Now that I've finally given in;
Given in to His knock on the door
Listening to Jesus forevermore
Oh… I'm learning something every day—
How to walk and how to pray
My life with Him has just begun
I'll fear no more—I know I've won
Yes… I know that I'm on Jesus's side;
There's no more stubbornness… no more pride.
I'll give to Him… my everything.
His praise and glory, I'll forever sing!
He has me in the palm of His hand
With special works and many great plans.
Oh… I'm learning something every day—
How to walk and how to pray
My life with Him has just begun
I'll fear no more—I know I've won
I've a plan to follow from dawn to dusk
In Jesus only—I'll put my trust
My eyes and heart now sparkle and shine—
Now that I've made Him totally mine!
Oh… I'll never go back to the days of my youth
For my new life is now… built on truth!

# Every Step You Take

Every step you take, I am
Protecting all of your ways
When you fully trust in Me
Each and every day

So be not afraid, oh, sinner
Oh come, come, come unto Me
Let the Savior of all the world
Fully welcome thee

To be among My flock
Through My gate you'll enter in
My favor shall be upon you
So come repent, give me your sins!

Oh, put it all down—
Let me heal and restore
Your heart, your soul
Come, come, my love is forevermore!

Come receive and believe
Follow Me, the light,
You'll be restored, and
You'll have new sight

So come unto Me
Be My son
I died for every man's sins
So will you please come?

# Hear My Tender Call

Hear My tender call
I am ever pleading for thee
To lift up your eyes
Be not ashamed to come to Me

I shall bring you to the Father
I'll plead before Him at all times
Crying out for mercy and grace
No matter your sins nor crime

I ever wait for you
To hear from the Son
Now is the time… don't wait
So come, oh, sinner, come

You'll never ever regret it
There's nothing you cannot tell Me
For on the Cross at Golgotha
I died for all, including thee

So come, be not ashamed
Come, come, and you shall see
Come, come, oh, sinner from afar
Come to the Savior, be set free

I'll teach you, I'll lead you
With My gentle staff in hand
I'll shepherd and lead you
Through valleys and rough lands

But I promise I Am with you
You'll ever be on My side
As you start your new journey
I'll teach and I will guide

# You Surround Me with Your Love

You surround me with Your love
Whatever the circumstance may be
Thank you for Your peace
and for never leaving me

You grace me with comfort through trials
for some unknown reason
You walk me through the valleys
and my lifetime seasons

Help me not lose patience
let Your peace be upon my face
As I watch Your hand move
the situations fall into place

With joy anew I draw strength
from You each new day
Thank You, Lord,
for always making a way

Yes, with heartfelt praise
and great thanksgiving
I thank You, Lord,
for another day of living

Though the trials are many
and the pain seems so much
I know I'll get through
with Your tender loving touch.

# The Journey in a Lifetime

Draw upon My wisdom,
Draw upon My peace;
Through My Living Spirit,
Your stressful cares will cease.

You'll know just how to handle
Each crisis that comes your way;
With My Spirit's strength,
Great peace is yours today.

The journey takes a lifetime,
So hold unto the Son;
Just when you think you're there,
He lets you know He's not done!

Yes, the journey is a lifetime,
So learn all you can;
Each new day you'll learn
To be with the great "I Am."

# God's Light Destroys Deception

My light destroys deception,
My discernment I will give;
I'll teach you how to discover,
How to truly live.

To be on guard every moment,
To detect the enemies' lies;
You'll know every trick
So you'll never ever deny...

The truth of My Word
Nor the plan I have for you,
You'll be strong and not afraid...
Wise in all you do.

# May People See and Know

O Lord, may people see and know to put their whole trust in You. Perhaps they have been half-hearted to the things of God. O Lord, wake them up, show them to put You first in all they do. May Your favor and blessings fall upon Your people as You teach how to fully trust, believe, and obey Your Word. May they live their lives and truly know how good You are.

This, O Lord, is just the beginning; help Your people to learn that You will never leave nor forsake them. Stir up Your gifts within them for creative ways of ingenuity to create new jobs and new skills. Help them to survive in these times. May Your Word and truth rise up within them. Give them ability to fully trust in You, along with the promises You have for them, as they obey and follow after You alone.

Amen.

# My Worn, Tattered Bible

My Bible's worn and tattered
With duct tape and Elmer's glue;
The pages are all crumpled,
But I call that "well used."

Now some say how pitiful a sight
To see that ragged, well-used book.
I know it looks just awful as
People gawk and look.

"Oh my goodness, girl,
You need a better-looking one.
How dare you use that ragged book?
You need a brand new one."

But this I tell you, friend,
I'd be lost without my Bible.
I can find everything I need—
And that makes me smile.

Because the pages are all wrinkled,
The pages are worn real thin,
But I don't really care about that.
It's very well used and makes God grin.

Because a messed-up old Bible
That is thirty-seven years old
Has all my favorite scriptures
With colored lines so bold!

All my lines of every color,
Some underlined twice or more,
Notes written all over them—
On pages and pages galore.

# Feeling Uprooted

Feeling uprooted
And on the road again?
Feeling unsettled
Every now and then?

Be not worried
It's part of My plan for you
Will you still follow Me
And stand true?

Changes are hard
But all a part of the game
And if you don't rebel
Much will be gained.

It brings forth fruit
Like you've never seen
Bright and beautiful
Fruit that just gleams.

Continue to trust Me
On the path so new
I will never
Misguide you.

# Set My Heart Aflame

Oh, fire of God
Set my heart aflame
I no longer want to run
Nor continue playing games—

I've neglected You so long
Cleanse my evil heart
Set my heart aflame
Give me a new start.

For I know in the past
I chose not to hear
Though I was aware
You were near.

Help me to make up
For all wasted time
Set my heart aflame
With your fire, Lord, refine…

All the days of my youth
My belligerent sins
Please forgive and guide me
Show me how to win—

Bring all my heart's darkness
Into your glorious light
Set my heart aflame, Lord
Make me righteous in Your sight.

Set my heart aflame again
That burns of only You
Set my heart aflame
That I may ever be true.

# Open Wide Your Ears

How good and gracious
Is our God?
Open wide your ears,
Oh, people,
Hear His voice
As He calls…

Praise and acknowledge Him,
For He calls you every day!
Know that His Word is true,
Learn to praise Him,
Giving Him the worship
Due His Name.

For His Word says that if
We don't praise Him, the
Very rocks will shout,
The trees of the land
Will clap their hands!

O God, how my heart
Sings with joy and
New hope fills my soul,
For You have brought me
From my deathbed
And have given me
New life…

# A Teachable Heart

Lord, I need Your loving direction
To stay on the path with You.
Help me stay on the narrow road,
The high calling of what is true.
Give me Your great wisdom,
Your sweet gentle ways.
Help my words to be of You
In all I think and say.
When I need correcting, Lord,
Give me ears to hear.
As You teach and correct me,
Help me ever to be near
To learn all I need to learn.
Through Your Spirit, teach me
That I may have a teachable heart
And ever glorify Thee.

# I'm in Need of Reconstruction

Endless tears both day and night,
I'm sure, by now, I look a fright!
Help me, Lord, I need some instruction,
I'm in great need of reconstruction!

Bursts of anger here and there,
How can I even ask for prayer
When I am always spouting out
Wrong spoken words and such doubt?

I know I should know better than I do.
Forgive me, Lord… I do love You,
But something's got a hold on me.
Help me, Lord, I want to be free.

Give me a Rhema word or two,
A Rhema word on which to chew.
O Lord, I truly want Your true will.
Why is it my mouth just spills?

Forth the negative and the sad,
How I hate it when I get this bad;
Help me refocus on your good,
For I know that I must and I should.

# Every Tender Word You Say

Every tender word you say
Brings My heart delight;
Just a glance, an inward smile,
To Me is a beautiful sight.

Give Me your heartfelt adoration,
Sing jubilant songs to Me,
Take refuge in My heart,
And soon you will see…

That I, your God,
I am your all,
I am always there for you
Before you even call.

So continue to adore Me
In all you say and do;
Look unto Me
As My blessings flow over you!

# I Will Ever Lead You Back Home

Listen to My voice
I'll lead your way
I Am all you need
You'll never be led astray

For I Am your Lord
Come to Me this hour
Great is My love,
Great is My power

Never walk the path
All alone—
I will ever lead you
Back home

# Hold Me Close to Your Heart, Lord

Hold me close to your heart, O Lord
Hold me 'til all fear is gone
Hold me just a bit longer
Sing to me a new song

Lift my spirit this moment
As I rest in Your arms today
Quiet my heavy heart, Lord
As You lead me Your way

Touch me deep in my spirit
As I let Your Word soak in me
Let all things that are troubling
Fully be set free

That I may be made whole again
As You hold me close to Your heart
So my day goes well, O Lord
With Your lift and a new start.

I love Thee, my Lord,
And all You do for me
Thank You for Your special touch
With new eyes I now see!

# Each New Day Is a Blessing

Each new day is a blessing
Help me to see that each day
Rather than the trials that come
My eyes will look your way

It's the little things in life
That means so much
Thank You, Lord Jesus,
For your lovely touch

And for all the
Special things You do
You're a wonderful God
Oh, how I love and worship You!

# It's Not What's on the Outside

It's not what's on the outside that counts;
It's only what comes from within.
You can look shiny on the outside
Yet inside darkened with sin!

Now you may think you can hide it,
But this, my friend, you must know,
That underneath the veneer so thin,
Others can see because it shows!

In time, you'll be found out
By the words you say.
Your character shall certainly
Give you away!

Because it's what's on the inside,
It's the only thing that counts, you see?
Don't play games with your soul's life,
Please listen to me.

Admit your sins,
Call on Jesus, ask Him in;
Repent of all wickedness,
Get rid of all your sins.

# When Daily Life Overwhelms Me

When the tests of daily life overwhelms me
And all hope seems to be gone
I look to the face of Jesus
And sing a hymn or song

I look to my sweet Jesus
You are my hiding place
With You beside me
There's nothing I can't face

For You are my blessed hope
In my joys and in my sorrows
As You fill me daily with Your joy
I've enough for all my tomorrows!

# With Intercession and Groans

Cry out in the Spirit
With intercessions and groans
Stand in the gap
Send prayers to My throne

It is a new day and season
I am doing a new thing
Refreshing My people
Great revivals I'll bring

Pray and you'll have favor
With Me and with man
In the midst of the happenings
You'll soon understand

That with Me you'll have
Nothing in life to fear
For My second coming
Will soon be here

So look up, look up
Walk in holiness today
Look to Jesus and
Follow His ways

# Live in the Hope of Tomorrow

Is your spirit
CRUSHED
and
BROKEN
BY
Things that
someone
said?
Then CHOOSE to
Not RECEIVE it
and
HOLD UP your HEAD!
Never take an
OFFENSE
or
DWELL
in the land
of
SORROW,
but
CHOOSE to LIVE
in
HOPE
And in the
GREAT EXPECTATION
of
TOMORROW!

# Doors of Opportunity

O God, my God
My merciful Savior
I pray to You
For great favor

That You may grant me
The desire of my heart
To walk with Thee daily
And never depart

From the path You chose
For this child of Yours
Thank You, Father
For opened doors…

Doors of opportunity
That no man can shut…
Doors no man can open—
No matter what!

# Recharge My Spiritual Battery

When my spiritual battery is running low
And my energy slowly seeping out,
When I'm tired, weak and weary
And my talking becomes a shout,
Then I know it's time for recharging.
My patience is running quite low
So lift me Lord, jumpstart me,
That I may continue to go
So I may be ever ready
For all Your plans for my day.
Recharge my spiritual battery
As I follow Your will and Your ways.
I promise to meet You in early morning
While it's still dark,
I'll find a solitary place
Praying before my day even starts.

# Rise Up, Stand Tall, and Don't Give Up

When you can't find your way
And doubtful of your course,
It's not time to quit
Or sit in remorse.
But rise up…
Stand tall…
And on the spirit depend
Call on God's word
And use it to defend.

The enemies and giants
And the mountainous hills
That comes against you
In God's perfect will.
Then as you trust the Lord
And as you obey,
Your problems will soon vanish
Like clouds that drift away.

# Fill Me, O Spirit

Continually fill me, O Spirit
Refresh me O Spirit, I pray
Give me new zeal and deeper love
Guide me in all of Your ways.

Fill me, Spirit, fill me
That I may be refreshed.
Give me more, O Spirit
I haven't enough of You yet.

Touch my spirit again,
Let me feel Your fire
Burning deep within my soul
For you're my burning desire.

# Though We Stumble

Though we blunder and stumble
In humanity
We stagger to rise
And wrestle continually.
Yet God, in all his wisdom,
Chose to live inside our hearts.
He chose to come into our lives
To set us apart.
Despite all of our failures and
All our darkened sins,
Christ shows each one of us
And shows us how to win.
Then in the growing process,
Old lusts and jealousies
Buried deep within our hearts
Can no longer be.
For his sweet residence
Deep within our soul
Continually renews us,
In him we're made
Completely whole.

# Keep Me from the Snares

O Lord, I call to you
Come quickly to me
Hear my voice, my calls
Come set me free.

For you are my refuge
I'm in desperate need
Rescue me, O Lord
Let those who pursue me
Not succeed.

Set me free of my flesh
And all my besetting sins
Set me free, O Lord
Let not my enemies win.

Keep me from the snares
They have laid for me.
Let them fall into their nets
While I pass by in safety.

# Drugs Destroy Lives

Drugs are such a tragedy  They destroy so many
lives.
Teenage boys and girls,
Men, women, husbands and wives.

The simple minded or intelligent
From every walk of life.
Both the young and old
All races, black or white.

O God, have mercy
On all of them today.
Lead, guide and deliver them,
Help them change their ways.

Draw them by Your spirit,
Give them new hope,
Spare their minds, O God,
Of the consequences of dope.

Turn their lives around
For the glory of Your son
That they may be a testimony
For the lost and lonely ones.

# Jesus Is Standing There with You

Discouragement, discouragement
Discouragements of the soul
Give them to the Lord
Let him make you whole.

All the trials that we encountered,
All the afflictions we go through,
Jesus Christ, the son of God,
Is standing there with you.

Comforting with his rod and staff
Through the dark shadows, he leads
For he is the great shepherd
Who meets all our needs.

So worry not about discouragement,
Take on no fear
Call upon the great shepherd
Who is ever near.

# I'm Only a Vessel

Like Paul, I am not perfect
I am only a vessel
A human vessel
Shaped by you, my Lord.

Inside this vessel,
I have within me Christ
The greatest treasure
His light, glory, love and
Compassion of heart.

Because of You, my Lord,
I have value
For in Your eyes
I am a new creature
Created in your likeness,
Who is being changed
From glory to glory
Each new day.

Thank you that I am pliable
In your hands
And obedient
To Your call.

# When Pain Strikes

Father God…
When pain strikes
And nothing man has made
Can take the severity of the pain away,
Reach down and help me, Lord,
To endure the suffering
Just as Your son, Jesus Christ, did
When he suffered horrendous pain
Yet he never whimpered nor uttered
An undesirable word against You
But instead, He took every throbbing,
Agonizing pain and endured it for me.
Help me to also bear the pain
And the suffering I have this day
Give me the grace and the strength
To endure, just as Jesus did for me
When He suffered and died that day.

# As We Quiet Our Spirits

May our trials
And struggles cease
As we quiet
Our hearts,
Seeking Your peace,
Refreshing our souls,
Keeping ourselves
From stress and
All strife.
O God, our refuge,
Our river of life,
Teach us to know
You alone, O God.
Teach us how to
Truly be still
Before You,
That we may
Follow and do
Your perfect will.
Touch our hearts
With Your
Flame of fire
That You alone
Are our one and
Only desire!
Amen.

# *References for Patricia Offerman Publishing*

Jordan-Barlow, R. (2002) *Daily in Your Presence Intimate Conversations with a Loving Father.* Uhrichsville, Ohio. Barbour Publishing. ISBN 1-58660-496-1.

Chambers, O. (1963) *My Utmost for His Highest.* Westwood, New Jersey. Barbour and Company, Inc. ISBN 1-55748-054 0.

*God Calling Journal.* (couldn't find the year printed) Uhrichsville, Ohio. Barbour Publishing. ISBN 1-55748-899-1.

Philpot, J. C. (1977) *Eats from Harvested Sheaves or Daily Portions.* Great Britain. Oxford University Press. Vivian Ridler, printer to the university. ISBN 0 903556 23 5.

Spurgeon, C. (1998) *Spurgeon on Prayer & Spiritual Warfare.* New Kensington, Pennsylvania. Whitaker House. ISBN 0-88368-527-2.

Spurgeon, C. (1991) *Morning and Evening Daily Readings.* United States of America. Hendrickson Publishers Inc. ISBN 0-943575-53-2.

Murray, A. (2007) *365 Daily Devotions on Prayer Inspiration on Talking with God.* Uhrichsville, Ohio. Barbour Publishing, Inc. ISBN 978-1-59789-866-9.

Kowalska, Saint Maria F. (2005) *Diary of Saint Maria Faustina Kowalska Divine Mercy in My Soul.* Stockbridge, Massachusetts. A Marian Press. ISBN 0-944203-04-3.

Bagster, S. (1999) *Daily Light on the Daily Path.* New Kensington, Pennsylvania. Whitaker House. ISBN 0-88368-556-6.

Jakes, T. D. (2004) *Devotional & Journal, 365 Days to Healing, Blessings, and Freedom.* Shippensburg, Pennsylvania. Destiny Image Publishers Inc. ISBN 0-7684-2969-2.

Willis, R. (2005) *A Daybook of Personal Moments with God When God Speaks to My Heart.* Lakeland, Florida. White Stone Books. ISBN 1-59379-042-2.

Cowman, C. E. (1980) *Springs in the Valley.* Minneapolis, Minnesota. World Wide Publications, A Ministry of the Billy Graham Association. ISBN 0-89066-031 X.

Spurgeon, C. (2004) Strengthen My Spirit *Daily Devotional Insights from the Writings of Charles Spurgeon.* Uhrichsville, Ohio. Barbour Publishing. ISBN 1 59310-373-5.

Domhue, A. C. (2001) *When I'm on My Knees Devotional Thoughts on Prayer for Women.* Uhrichsville, Ohio. Barbour Publishing. ISBN 1-58660-564-X.

Steiner-Rice, H. (Year unknown) *Loving Promises Especially for You.* Carmel, New York. ExLibris. ISBN, unable to find in book/front page missing.

Barlow-Jordan, R. (2002) *Daily in Your Presence.* Uhrichsville, Ohio. Barbour Publishing. ISBN 1-59310-024-8.

Thompson, F. C., PhD. (1982) *The Thompson Chain Reference Bible New International Version.* Grand Rapids, Michigan. Zondervan Bible Publishers.

www.ingramcontent.com/pod-product-compliance
Lightning Source LLC
Chambersburg PA
CBHW022214050726
47590CB00002B/785